Gold Stars®

Maths

AGES **9-11** KEY STAGE 2

PaRragon

Bath · New York · Cologne · Melbourne · Delhi
Hong Kong · Shenzhen · Singapore

This edition published by Parragon Books Ltd in 2018

Parragon Books Ltd
Chartist House
15–17 Trim Street
Bath BA1 1HA, UK
www.parragon.com

Written by Paul Broadbent
Educational consultants: Martin Malcolm and Catherine Casey
Illustrated by Rob Davis/www.the-art-agency.co.uk
and Tom Connell/www.the-art-agency.co.uk

ISBN 978-1-5270-0237-1

Printed in China

arents' not s

The Gold Stars Key Stage 2 series

The Gold Stars Key Stage 2 series has been created to help your child practise key skills and information learned in school. Each book has been written by an expert team of teachers. This book will help your child to consolidate key skills in Maths, helping to develop confidence and understanding of these topics.

How to use this workbook

- Talk through the introductions to each topic and review the examples together.

- Encourage your child to tackle the fill-in activities independently.

- Keep work times short. Skip a page if it seems too difficult and return to it later.

- It doesn't matter if your child does some of the pages out of order.

- Your child may need some extra scrap paper for working out on some of the pages.

- Check the answers on pages 60-63. Encourage effort and reward achievement with praise.

- If your child finds any of the pages too difficult, don't worry. Children learn at different rates.

Contents

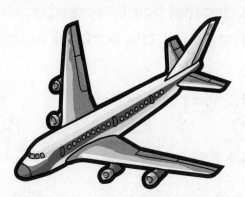

Decimals

Learning objective: to read whole numbers and decimals

A decimal point separates whole numbers from decimal fractions - the parts of numbers that are less than 1.

> Decimals are often used to show the price of things.

Numbers use ten digits.

0   1   2   3   4   5   6   7   8   9

Look at this number.

37.842

3 tens	7 units	8 tenths	4 hundredths	2 thousandths
(30)	(7)	$\frac{8}{10}$	$\frac{4}{100}$	$\frac{2}{1000}$

This is read as thirty-seven point eight four two.

A Write the decimal number each arrow points to.

1. _____   2. _____   3. _____   4. _____

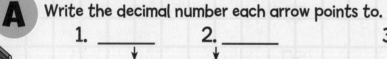

0   0.1   0.2   0.3   0.4   0.5   0.6   0.7   0.8   0.9   1

5. _____   6. _____   7. _____   8. _____   9. _____

8   8.1   8.2   8.3   8.4   8.5   8.6   8.7   8.8   8.9   9

10. _____   11. _____   12. _____   13. _____   14. _____

16   16.1 16.2 16.3 16.4 16.5 16.6 16.7 16.8 16.9 17

B

This table shows the weight in kilograms of some of the turtles that swim in our seas. Write the list in order of weight, starting with the heaviest.

Turtle	Weight (kilograms)	Turtle	Weight (kilograms)
Flatback turtle	78.151		
Green sea turtle	355.3		
Hawksbill turtle	62.65		
Kemp's Ridley turtle	60.45		
Leatherback turtle	462.9		
Loggerhead turtle	257.801		

C

Rearrange this set of digits to make 6 different decimal numbers between 1 and 10. Use each digit only once in each decimal number.

1.

___.___ ___.___ ___.___ ___.___ ___.___ ___.___

2. Write the decimal numbers you have made in order, starting with the smallest.

__.___ __.___ __.___ __.___ __.___ __.___

smallest →

lace valu

The position of a digit in a number shows what the number is worth.
This is what we mean by place value.

Making a number 10 times bigger or smaller is easy if you follow these rules.

To multiply any number by 10:
Move the digits one place to the left.

x10

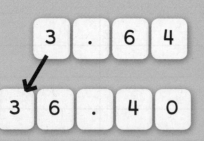

To divide any number by 10:
Move the digits one place to the right.

÷10

A Answer these.

1. 1.35 x 10 = ~~10.035~~   2. 9.675 x 10 = _____

3. 68.5 ÷ 10 = _____   4. 334.6 ÷ 10 = _____

B Read and answer these.

1.
A bucket holds
3.5 litres of water.
How much water
would there be in 10
buckets?

_____

2.
A car travels a total
of 9.852km each
day. How far does
the car travel after
10 days?

_____

3.
A 250kg sack of
grain is divided into
10 packs. How much
does each pack of
grain weigh?

_____

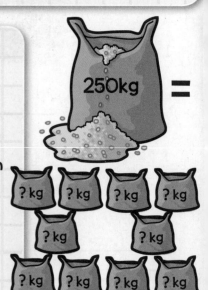

8

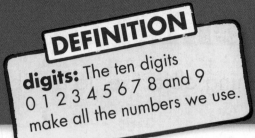

DEFINITION

digits: The ten digits 0 1 2 3 4 5 6 7 8 and 9 make all the numbers we use.

This is a super-square:

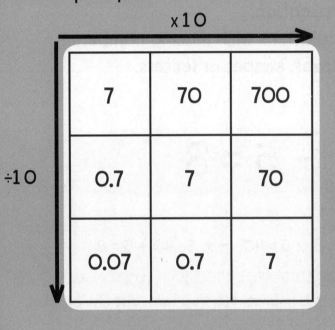

	×10	
7	70	700
0.7	7	70
0.07	0.7	7

÷10

Putting a zero on the end of a decimal number does not change the number. 3.8 is the same as 3.80!

C

Complete these super-squares.

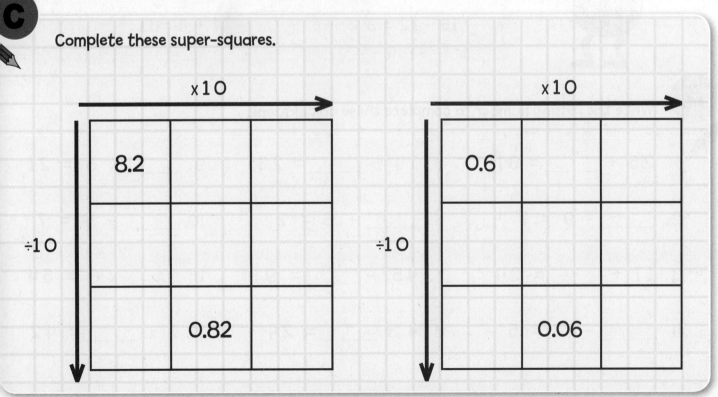

	×10	
8.2		
	0.82	

÷10

	×10	
0.6		
	0.06	

÷10

9

Mentul calculation

Learning objective: to be able to calculate mentally and use brackets

Subtraction is the inverse or opposite of addition.
Division is the inverse or opposite of multiplication.
Use these facts to help you work out calculations with missing numbers.
Missing numbers can be represented by boxes, shapes or letters.

Knowing your multiplication tables and addition bonds is important.

$$\_\_\_\_ \div 5 = 8$$

Use multiplication:

$8 \times 5 = \_\_\_\_$ → $8 \times 5 = 40$ → So $40 \div 5 = 8$

When part of a problem is in brackets, you work out the bracket part first.

$15 - (8 + 4) = \_\_\_\_$ $(15 - 8) + 4 = \_\_\_\_$

$15 - 12 = 3$ $7 + 4 = 11$

A

Write the missing number to complete these calculations.

1. $25 + \_\_\_\_ = 31$

2. $\_\_\_\_ - 9 = 7$

3. $17 + \_\_\_\_ = 24$

4. $\_\_\_\_ - 13 = 5$

5. $14 + \_\_\_\_ = 23$

6. $\_\_\_\_ \div 6 = 2$

7. $45 \div \_\_\_\_ = 9$

8. $4 \times \_\_\_\_ = 24$

9. $\_\_\_\_ \times 3 = 21$

10. $\_\_\_\_ \div 9 = 7$

11. $\_\_\_\_ \times 6 = 54$

12. $7 \times \_\_\_\_ = 42$

B

Write the answer for each of these. Remember to work out the brackets first.

1. (19 − 3) + 4 = _____

2. 14 − (7 + 2) = _____

3. (13 − 5) x 2 = _____

4. 16 − (8 − 3) = _____

5. 3 x (9 − 5) = _____

6. (4 + 6) ÷ 2 = _____

7. (8 + 2) − (3 + 5) = _____

8. (9 x 3) + (4 x 5) = _____

C

Draw brackets to make each answer 12.

1. 19 − 12 − 5

2. 16 − 10 − 6

3. 22 − 5 + 5

4. 6 + 13 − 7

5. 24 − 6 − 6

6. 20 − 10 − 2

Try using opposite calculations to find the number.

D

What's my number?
Work out the mystery number for each of these.

1. When I divide my number by 6 the answer is 8.   ____

2. When I multiply my number by 6 the answer is 42.   ____

3. When I double my number and then add 3 the answer is 19.   ____

4. When I divide my number by 3 and then add 5 the answer is 12.   ____

5. When I multiply my number by 5 and then subtract 6 the answer is 39.   ____

6. When I divide my number by 4 and then subtract 2 the answer is 3.   ____

Make up your own mystery number puzzles like this.

11

Square numbers

When two identical whole numbers are multiplied together they make a square number.

1 x 1 = 1
1 squared = 1
$1^2 = 1$

2 x 2 = 4
2 squared = 4
$2^2 = 4$

3 x 3 = 9
3 squared = 9
$3^2 = 9$

4 x 4 = 16
4 squared = 16
$4^2 = 16$

The numbers 1, 4, 9 and 16 are examples of square numbers.

A Write the missing numbers to complete this multiplication table.

	0	1	2	3	4	5	6	7	8	9	10	11	12
0	0	0		0	0			0	0		0		
1			2			5	6	7		9	10		
2	0		4	6	8				16	18			
3		3		9	12		18	21				33	
4	0								32				
5				15	20		30			45			60
6													
7	0	7											
8		8		24		40		56		72			
9	0									81			
10		10			40				80		100		
11				33									
12											120		

B

Colour the square for each of these in the multiplication table opposite.

1x1 2x2 3x3 4x4 5x5 6x6 7x7 8x8 9x9 10x10 11x11 12x12

What do you notice?

C

Circle the numbers in each set that are not square numbers.

1. 36   24   16   64   48

2. 25   81   9   15   12

3. 1   100   46   4   49

4. 18   49   9   81   77

5. 36   6   4   64   50

6. 49   9   39   100   92

Read across and down to multiply 2 numbers together. If you go across from 5 and down from 4 it meets at 20. So 5 x 4 = 20 and 4 x 5 = 20!

D

Answer these.

1. $4^2 =$ _____
2. $7^2 =$ _____
3. $6^2 =$ _____
4. $9^2 =$ _____
5. $12^2 =$ _____

6. $2^2 =$ _____
7. $10^2 =$ _____
8. $3^2 =$ _____
9. $8^2 =$ _____
10. $5^2 =$ _____

Multiples and factors

Learning objective: to identify pairs of factors and find common multiples

A multiple of a whole number is produced by multiplying that number by another whole number. Factors of a number can divide that number exactly.

Multiples of 3 →	3	6	9	12	15	18	21	24
Multiples of 4 →	4	8	12	16	20	24	28	32

12 is a multiple of both 3 and 4.
This means that 12 is a common multiple of 3 and 4.

10 has 4 factors because it can only be divided exactly by 4 numbers.

$10 \div 1 = 10$
$10 \div 2 = 5$
$10 \div 5 = 2$
$10 \div 10 = 1$

Factors of 10 in order: 1, 2, 5, 10
Factors of 10 in pairs: (1, 10) (2, 5)

Factors divide a number exactly.

Multiples mean more for me!

A Write all the pairs of factors for each of these numbers.

1. 8

(__,__)   (__,__)

2. 20

(__,__)   (__,__)

(__,__)

3. 24

(__,__)   (__,__)

(__,__)   (__,__)

4. 28

(__,__)   (__,__)

(__,__)

14

B

Write the first 10 multiples for each of these numbers.

1. multiples of 4 → ___ ___ ___ ___ ___ ___ ___ ___ ___ ___
2. multiples of 3 → ___ ___ ___ ___ ___ ___ ___ ___ ___ ___
3. multiples of 6 → ___ ___ ___ ___ ___ ___ ___ ___ ___ ___
4. multiples of 5 → ___ ___ ___ ___ ___ ___ ___ ___ ___ ___
5. multiples of 10 → ___ ___ ___ ___ ___ ___ ___ ___ ___ ___
6. multiples of 8 → ___ ___ ___ ___ ___ ___ ___ ___ ___ ___

C

Look at your answers for Exercise B. Use the lists of multiples to help you find the common multiples for each of these pairs of numbers.

1. 3 and 5 → _____ _____
2. 4 and 3 → _____ _____
3. 4 and 5 → _____ _____

4. 6 and 8 → _____ _____
5. 10 and 6 → _____ _____
6. 6 and 4 → _____ _____ _____

D

Write these numbers in the correct part of the Venn diagram.

12 4 18
10 24 16
15 3 20
9 6 25
2 30 1

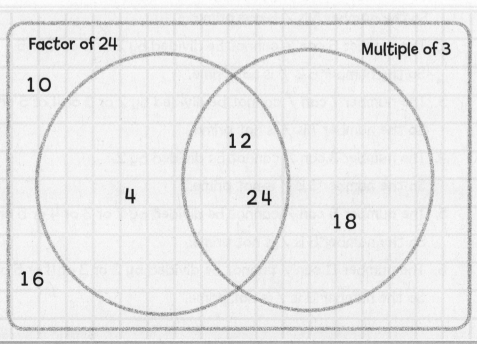

Factor of 24   Multiple of 3

10

12

4   24

18

16

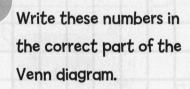

15

Prime numbers

Prime numbers are special. You cannot divide them exactly by any other smaller number.

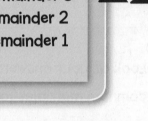

The only even prime number is 2. The other primes are all odd!

not prime

12 divides exactly by all these numbers . . .

$12 \div 2 = 6$
$12 \div 3 = 4$
$12 \div 4 = 3$
$12 \div 6 = 2$

prime

But 13 just won't divide exactly . . .

$13 \div 2 = 6$ remainder 1 $13 \div 8 = 1$ remainder 5
$13 \div 3 = 4$ remainder 1 $13 \div 9 = 1$ remainder 4
$13 \div 4 = 3$ remainder 1 $13 \div 10 = 1$ remainder 3
$13 \div 5 = 2$ remainder 3 $13 \div 11 = 1$ remainder 2
$13 \div 6 = 2$ remainder 1 $13 \div 12 = 1$ remainder 1
$13 \div 7 = 1$ remainder 6

A

Cross out the words to show the primes. The first two have been done for you.

Odd but true – maths experts say the number 1 doesn't count as a prime number!

1. The number 5 ~~can~~ / cannot be divided by 2 or 3 or 4.
   So the number 5 is / ~~is not~~ prime.
2. The number 6 can / ~~cannot~~ be divided by 2 or 3 ~~or 4 or 5~~.
   So the number 6 ~~is~~ / is not prime.
3. The number 7 can / cannot be divided by 2 or 3 or 4 or 5 or 6.
   So the number 7 is / is not prime.
4. The number 3 can / cannot be divided by 2.
   So the number 3 is / is not prime.
5. The number 8 can / cannot be divided by 2 or 3 or 4 or 5 or 6 or 7.
   So the number 8 is / is not prime.
6. The number 11 can / cannot be divided by 2 or 3 or 4 or 5 or 6 or 7 or 8 or 9 or 10.
   So the number 11 is / is not prime.

DEFINITION

prime number: A whole number bigger than 1, that can't be exactly divided by any other whole number.

B

All the numbers in the green box can be divided by 2, 3 or 5 . . .

except for the prime numbers. Circle six more hidden primes.

15	48	25	(7)	18	44
62	11	20	12	36	
50	14	6	22	13	75
30	17	16	10	4	
90	26	24	27	33	19
100	35	55	60	8	
70	9	23	16	21	22
29	86	64	85	40	

C

This poem helps you remember all the prime numbers up to 20.

Fill in the missing rhymes.

| **missing rhymes** |
| seventeen   two |
| eleven   nineteen |
| five   thirteen |

They can't be divided, whatever you do

The smallest prime is number _____

Then come three and _____ and seven

The next prime is of course _____

_____ is next upon the scene

_____ follows and then _____.

Written addition

Learning objective: to use efficient written methods to add whole numbers

When you add numbers like this, it helps to line up the columns. If a column adds up to 10 or more, carry the 10 over to the next column by writing a small number 1 beneath. Then add it with the numbers in that column.

The columns are: thousands, hundreds, tens and units.

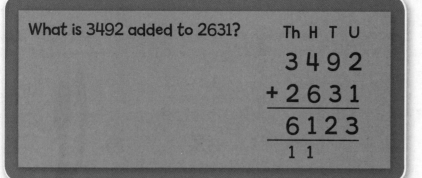

What is 3492 added to 2631?

```
  Th H T U
     3 4 9 2
  +  2 6 3 1
  ─────────
     6 1 2 3
        1 1
```

Look out for addition words in problems: add, total, sum, altogether, greater than...

A Answer these.

1.
```
   6 7 2 8
 + 2 7 4 0
```

2.
```
   3 1 2 8
 + 4 6 7 5
```

3.
```
   1 5 6 1
 + 2 9 1 8
```

B Read and answer these. Use a pen and paper to work out each calculation.

1. Add together 3945 and 5680. _____

2. What is 5929 and 3874 added together? _____

3. What is the sum of 2263 and 3815? _____

4. Total 5923 and 1946. _____

5. What is the total of 4328 and 2749? _____

6. What number is 4444 greater than 1991? _____

C

Look at these distances and work out the different totals.

A ➞ 1652km   B ➞ 3559km   C ➞ 3081km   D ➞ 2722 km   E ➞ 1768km

1. A + E   ➞ _____ km

2. D + C   ➞ _____ km

3. B + D   ➞ _____ km

4. C + E   ➞ _____ km

5. E + D   ➞ _____ km

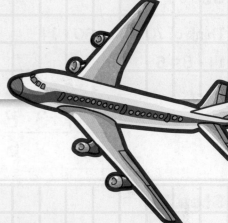

D

All the digits 1 and 3 are missing.

Write the digits 1 or 3 in the correct place to complete this addition.

```
    4 6 □ 8
  +
      9 □ 6 □
    ─────────
    □ □ 8 0 □
```

Use your knowledge of place value.

Write the numbers 1 and 3 on six small pieces of paper and try them in the different missing boxes to see which ones work.

Written subtraction

Learning objective: to use efficient written methods to subtract whole numbers

There are different ways of taking one number away from another.
If you can't work it out in your head you can try a written method.

Example
What is 3674 subtract 1738?

Step 1

Think of 70 + 4 as 60 + 14

14 - 8 = 6

$$3\ 6\ ^6\!7\ ^1\!4$$
$$-1\ 7\ 3\ 8$$
$$\underline{6}$$

Step 2

60 - 30 = 30

$$3\ 6\ ^6\!7\ ^1\!4$$
$$-1\ 7\ 3\ 8$$
$$\underline{3\ 6}$$

Make sure you line up the columns correctly.

Step 3

Think of 3000 + 600 as 2000 + 1600.

1600 - 700 = 900

$$^2\!3\ ^1\!6\ ^6\!7\ ^1\!4$$
$$-1\ 7\ 3\ 8$$
$$\underline{9\ 3\ 6}$$

Step 4

2000 - 1000 = 1000

$$^2\!3\ ^1\!6\ ^6\!7\ ^1\!4$$
$$-1\ 7\ 3\ 8$$
$$\underline{1\ 9\ 3\ 6}$$

A Write the answers.

1.
$$4\ 7\ 3\ 8$$
$$-1\ 5\ 9\ 2$$

2.
$$9\ 4\ 7\ 1$$
$$-3\ 8\ 0\ 3$$

3.
$$6\ 5\ 4\ 5$$
$$-2\ 1\ 7\ 5$$

DEFINITION

subtraction: Taking one number away from another. The - sign shows one number is being taken away from another.

B

Write the missing digits in these subtractions.

1.
```
    3  8  4  ☐
  - 1  7  ☐  2
  ───────────
    2  ☐  8  5
```

2.
```
    7  ☐  4  3
  - 2  4  8  ☐
  ───────────
    ☐  4  5  7
```

3.
```
    4  1  1  5
  - 2  ☐  3  ☐
  ───────────
    ☐  1  7  9
```

C

This table shows the depths of the deepest oceans and seas in the world.

Look at the table and answer the questions.

Ocean/sea	Average depth (metres)
Pacific Ocean	4028m
Indian Ocean	3963m
Atlantic Ocean	3926m
Caribbean Sea	2647m
South China Sea	1652m
Bering Sea	1547m
Gulf of Mexico	1486m
Mediterranean Sea	1429m

1. How much deeper is the Caribbean Sea than the Gulf of Mexico?

2. By how many metres is the Pacific Ocean deeper than the Caribbean Sea?

3. What is the difference in depth between the Atlantic Ocean and the Caribbean Sea?

4. Which two seas have a difference in depth of 1100m?

5. Which sea is 1316m less in depth than the Indian Ocean?

6. Which two oceans or seas have the smallest difference in depth?

21

Written multiplication

Learning objective: to use written methods to multiply
TU (tens and units) x TU

When you need to multiply two numbers together, decide whether you can work out the answer in your head, or whether you need to use a written method.

Look at these two written methods for 34 x 26.

Method 1

x	30	4		
20	600	80	→	680
6	180	24	→	+ 204
				884

Method 2

```
    34
  x 26
  204   (34 x 6)
  680   (34 x 20)
  884
```

It is always a good idea to estimate the answer first and then check your final answer with your estimate.

A Complete these multiplications.

1. 1 9 x 7 6 = _____

2. 8 4 x 3 7 = _____

3.
```
      1 9
    x 2 4
```

4.
```
      5 3
    x 6 2
```

22

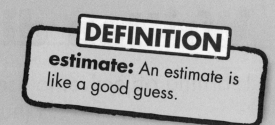

DEFINITION

estimate: An estimate is like a good guess.

B Read and answer these questions.

1. There are 24 hours in a day. How many hours are there in September? _____

2. A truck makes a 58km journey 16 times in a week. How far does the truck travel in total? _____

3. A packet of nuts weighs 28g and there are 25 packets in a box. How many grams of nuts are there in a full box? _____

4. There are 15 pencils in a pack and a school orders 49 packs. How many pencils will there be altogether? _____

C This is an order form for equipment for a school.

How many of each item has been ordered?

Items	Amount in 1 pack	Number of packs	Total number of items
Pencils	28	76	
Chalk	15	33	
Sharpeners	26	19	
Erasers	48	14	
Pens	52	58	
Crayons	34	47	

D Write the digits 3, 4, 5 and 6 on small pieces of paper.

Using all 4 digits, arrange the numbers to make different multiplications.

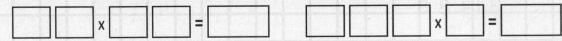

☐☐ x ☐☐ = ☐☐☐   ☐☐☐ x ☐ = ☐☐☐☐

1. What is the largest answer you can make?
2. What is the smallest answer?
3. What answer is the nearest you can make to 1000?

Written division

Some dividing you can do in your head as it links with multiplying. 48 divided by 6 is 8, which is easy if you know that 6 x 8 is 48. When you divide bigger numbers, you need to use a written method.

Remember!
If a number cannot be divided exactly it leaves a remainder.

What is 749 divided by 4?

Work out how many groups of 4 are in 749 and what is left over:

Method 1

```
       187 r1
   4)749
    -400     (4 x 100)
     349
    -320     (4 x 80)
      29
     -28     (4 x 7)      749 ÷ 4 = 187 remainder 1
       1
```

Method 2

```
       187 r1
   4)7³4²9
```

$700 ÷ 4 = 100$
Carry 300 over to the tens.
$340 ÷ 4 = 80$
Carry 20 over to the units.
$29 ÷ 4 = 7$
The remainder is 1.

A   Complete these divisions and write the answers with remainders.

1. $488 ÷ 3$ → _____ r__   3. $189 ÷ 4$ → _____ r__
       3)488   4)189

2. $367 ÷ 5$ → _____ r__   4. $926 ÷ 4$ → _____ r__
       5)367   4)926

DEFINITION

remainder: If a number cannot be divided exactly by another number then there is a whole number answer with an amount left over, called a remainder.

Use paper for written workings out.

B Draw a line to match each remainder to a division.

271 ÷ 6

315 ÷ 8

454 ÷ 5

608 ÷ 3

Remainder
1
2
3
4
5
6
7
8
9

149 ÷ 6

259 ÷ 9

359 ÷ 10

458 ÷ 9

398 ÷ 7

C

Eggs are collected every day and put into boxes of 6. Write how many full boxes can be made each day and how many eggs are left over to complete this chart.

Day of the week	Eggs collected	Number of	
		Full boxes (6 eggs)	**Eggs left over**
Monday	627		
Tuesday	572		
Wednesday	700		
Thursday	644		
Friday	683		
Saturday	594		
Sunday	735		

Algebra

Learning objective: to use a simple formula and express a problem algebraically

In algebra, letters are used to represent numbers.

For example:

If $a = 3$ $b = 6$ $c = 4$

$a + b = 3 + 6 = 9$ $b - c = 6 - 4 = 2$

$ab = 3 \times 6 = 18$ $\frac{a}{b} = \frac{3}{6} = \frac{1}{2}$

In algebra, we think of the numbers on either side of the equals sign as a balance scale. The scale has to stay balanced, so whatever you do to one side you have to do to the other side too.

To find out what the value of **a** is in the algebra problem below, we need to remove the +40 to isolate the **a**.

For example:

$a + 40 = 100$
$a + 40 - 40 = 100 - 40$
$a = 60$

The inverse of + 40 is - 40, so we take 40 away from both sides of the equals sign.

A

Find the value of **a** in each of these problems. Use the space on the right or a separate piece of paper for your workings out.

1. $a + 30 = 100$

   $a =$

2. $a + 20 = 80$

   $a =$

3. $a - 40 = 120$

   $a =$

4. $a - 100 = 150$

   $a =$

a has a different value in each problem!

algebra: A type of maths that uses letters in place of numbers. A letter can represent any number.

Algebra problems also use multiplying and dividing. To find out the value of **c** in the algebra problem below, we need to remove the x6.

For example:

$$c \times 6 = 24$$
$$c \times 6 \div 6 = 24 \div 6$$
$$c = 4$$

The inverse of x 6 is ÷ 6, so we divide both sides of the equals sign by 6.

B

Find the value of **b** in each of these problems. Use the space on the right or a separate piece of paper for your workings out.

Remember!
Addition and subtraction are inverses, and multiplication and division are inverses.

1. b X 12 = 48

   b =

2. b X 30 = 120

   b =

3. b ÷ 8 = 9

   b =

4. b ÷ 10 = 15

   b =

C

Solve these two algebra problems. Use the space on the right or a separate piece of paper for your workings out.

In algebra, we write **2 X n** as **2n**.

1. n = 20

   What is 2n + 9? _____

2. 2q + 4 = 10

   What is the value of q? _____

Learning objective: to use rounding and approximation to estimate calculations

We round numbers to make them easier to work with. It is useful for estimating approximate, or rough, answers.

Decimal numbers can be rounded to the nearest whole number or tenth. Whole numbers can be rounded to the nearest 10, 100 or 1000. Round down if the digit is less than 5. Round up if the digit is 5 or more.

To round decimals to the nearest whole number, look at the **tenth** digit.

4.**4**7 round down to 4
12.**7**5 round up to 13

To round numbers to the nearest 10, look at the **units** digit.

2**4** round down to 20
8**5** round up to 90

To round large numbers to the nearest 100, look at the **tens** digit.

68**2**8 round down to 6800
304**5**9 round up to 30500

To round large numbers to the nearest 1000, look at the **hundreds** digit.

68**4**28 round down to 68000
304**6**59 round up to 305000

A This chart shows some cities with a population of less than 1 million. Round each population to the nearest 100.

Tip: focus on the last 3 digits in each number.

Town	Population	Nearest 100
Liverpool	469019	
Bradford	293717	
Sheffield	439866	
Derby	229407	
Birmingham	970892	
Nottingham	249584	
Bristol	420556	
Plymouth	243795	

B

Round each number to the nearest 100, then do the sum.

1. 415 + 388 → _____   4. 378 + 836 → _____

2. 682 - 174 → _____   5. 2190 + 3675 → _____

3. 597 - 489 → _____   6. 9251 + 4359 → _____

C

Round each of these to the nearest whole number of kilograms. Write the approximate total weights for each set.

1.	4.38 kg	2.97 kg	9.19 kg	Approx. total weight _____ kg
2.	9.49 kg	7.73 kg	3.64 kg	Approx. total weight _____ kg
3.	13.85 kg	12.55 kg	6.53 kg	Approx. total weight _____ kg
4.	19.09 kg	17.64 kg	8.47 kg	Approx. total weight _____ kg

D

Calculators can display lots of decimal places.

We often round off numbers to 2 decimal places.

0.76398	→ rounds down to	0.76
3.42739	→ rounds up to	3.43

Round these to 2 decimal places.

1. 0.9286 _____   2. 7.0835 _____   3. 12.945 _____

4. 7.5881 _____   5. 2.9116 _____   6. 30.0794 _____

29

Decimal calculations

Learning objective: to use written methods to add
and subtract decimals

Some decimals you can add and subtract in your head, but other bigger
numbers will need a written method.

Adding and subtracting decimals is just like adding and subtracting whole numbers. Just
remember that the decimal point in the answer is in line with the decimal points above.

Example 1
What is 12.78 added to 37.41?

An approximate answer is 13 + 37 = 50

```
   12.78
+  37.41
   50.19
    1 1
```

Example 2
What is 34.82 subtract 19.96?

An approximate answer is 35 – 20 = 15

```
 ²3 ¹³4 . ¹⁷8 ¹2
-  1 9 . 9 6
   1 4 . 8 6
```

A Complete these additions.

1. 45.37
  + 22.46

2. 31.85
  + 52.91

3. 73.02
  + 18.79

4. 64.89
  + 20.62

B Complete these subtractions.

1. 77.86
  – 34.84

2. 90.52
  – 43.29

3. 65.19
  – 27.43

4. 58.03
  – 16.25

It is always a good idea to estimate an
approximate answer first, so you can
check your answer against your estimate.

DEFINITION

difference: The difference between two numbers is the amount by which one number is greater than the other. The difference between 18 and 21 is 21 − 18 = 3.

C

Write the total measurements.

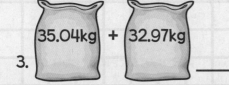

1. 13.88l + 12.75l _____

2. 47.39m + 16.52m _____

3. 35.04kg + 32.97kg _____

4. 59.87m + 21.36m _____

D

This chart shows the gymnasts' scores for four events. Using information from the chart answer the questions below.

Name	Horse Vault	Uneven Bars	Balance Beam	Floor Exercise
Eileen	18.10	19.16	18.96	19.36
Sandra	18.40	19.40	19.02	19.00
Nikki	19.16	18.89	18.66	18.96
Julie	19.19	19.26	19.13	19.20
Stacey	19.03	18.99	19.22	18.70

1. What is the difference between the Horse Vault scores of Sandra and Nikki?

2. What is the difference between the highest and lowest scores on the Uneven Bars?

3. Which two gymnasts have a difference of 0.4 in their Floor Exercise scores?

4. How many more points did Julie need on the Balance Beam to match the top score for this event?

5. The scores were each out of 20. How far from full marks was Nikki on the Balance Beam?

31

Fractions

Learning objective: to simplify, add and subtract fractions

With some fractions, it's hard to picture exactly what they mean.

The numerator (the number on the top) and the denominator (the number on the bottom) are both bigger than they need to be. Like this:

$$\frac{20}{25}$$

You can make fractions like this simpler and easier to understand if you can spot a number that divides both the numerator and denominator.

$20 \div 5 = 4$
$25 \div 5 = 5$

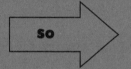 so

$\frac{20}{25}$ is the same as $\frac{4}{5}$

You must use the same number to divide the top and bottom of the fraction.

A

Find the right number to simplify each fraction.

1. $15 \div \underline{} = $
   $40 \div \underline{} = $
   so $\frac{15}{40}$ is the same as $\underline{}$

2. $14 \div \underline{} = $
   $16 \div \underline{} = $
   so $\frac{14}{16}$ is the same as $\underline{}$

3. $8 \div \underline{} = $
   $12 \div \underline{} = $
   so $\frac{8}{12}$ is the same as $\underline{}$

4. $20 \div \underline{} = $
   $30 \div \underline{} = $
   so $\frac{20}{30}$ is the same as $\underline{}$

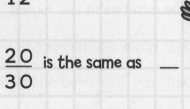

Hint: all even numbers divide by 2. All numbers that end with 0 divide by 10. And all numbers that end with 0 or 5 divide by 5.

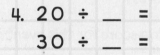

Add or subtract fractions with the same denominator by adding or subtracting the numerators. If fractions have different denominators, look to see how to make the denominators the same before adding or subtracting the numerators.

Example 1

$$\frac{4}{7} + \frac{5}{7} = \frac{9}{7} = 1\frac{2}{7}$$

The denominators are the same, so there is no need to do anything to them.

Example 2

$$\frac{2}{3} + \frac{1}{6} = \frac{2 \times 2}{3 \times 2} + \frac{1}{6} = \frac{4}{6} + \frac{1}{6} = \frac{5}{6}$$

We make the denominators the same by multiplying the top and bottom of the first fraction by 2.

Example 3

$$\frac{2}{3} - \frac{1}{2} = \frac{2 \times 2}{3 \times 2} - \frac{1 \times 3}{2 \times 3} = \frac{4}{6} - \frac{3}{6} = \frac{1}{6}$$

We make the denominators the same by multiplying the first fraction by 2 and the second fraction by 3.

B Try these

1. $\dfrac{5}{9} + \dfrac{8}{9} =$ —— = ——

2. $\dfrac{7}{10} + \dfrac{8}{10} =$ —— = —— = ——

C Try these. Don't forget to simplify your answers if you can.

1. $\dfrac{1}{3} + \dfrac{1}{9} =$

2. $\dfrac{3}{7} + \dfrac{1}{14} =$

3. $\dfrac{1}{3} + \dfrac{1}{2} =$

4. $\dfrac{1}{2} + \dfrac{3}{5} =$

5. $\dfrac{7}{9} - \dfrac{1}{3} =$

6. $\dfrac{2}{3} - \dfrac{1}{4} =$

Whatever you do to the bottom number of a fraction, you do the same to the top number.

33

Equivalents

Learning objective: to find equivalent percentages, decimals and fractions

When something is part of a whole, it can be displayed as a fraction, decimal or percentage.

Look at this grid.
25% of the grid is red.

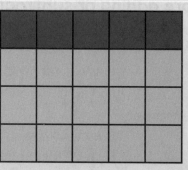

$$\frac{5}{20} = \frac{25}{100} = 25\%$$

25% is the same as $\frac{1}{4}$.

Look at these methods for converting between fractions, percentages and decimals:

Per cent to decimal

Divide the percentage by 100

Example: 60% is the same as 0.6

Decimal to per cent

Multiply the decimal by 100

Example: 0.25 is the same as 25%

Per cent to fraction

Write the percentage as a fraction out of 100 and then simplify

Example: 40% is $\frac{40}{100}$, which is the same as $\frac{2}{5}$

Fraction to per cent

Write the fraction as a decimal and then multiply by 100

Example: $\frac{3}{4}$ is 0.75 which is the same as 75%

A 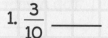 Use the methods shown above to change these fractions and decimals to percentages.

Turn to page 6 for revision on decimals.

1. $\frac{3}{10}$ _____   2. $\frac{1}{5}$ _____   3. $\frac{7}{100}$ _____   4. $\frac{11}{50}$ _____

5. 0.8 _____   6. 0.1 _____   7. 0.65 _____   8. 0.12 _____

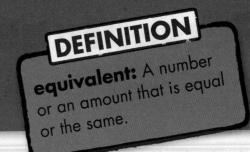

DEFINITION

equivalent: A number or an amount that is equal or the same.

B Write the missing digits to complete these.

1. $\frac{1}{2}$ = 0._____ = 50%

2. $\frac{1}{4}$ = 0.25 = _____%

3. $\frac{1}{20}$ = 0.05 = _____%

4. $\frac{2}{\boxed{}}$ = 0.4 = 40%

5. $\frac{17}{50}$ = 0._____ = 34%

6. $\frac{7}{10}$ = 0.7 = _____%

C Write the fraction and percentage shown by the shaded part of each shape.

1.

2.

3.

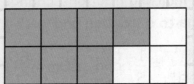

4.

5.

6.

D Write the percentages for each of these headlines.

1. There was a one-in-a-hundred chance of finding the treasure.

   There was a _____% chance of finding the treasure.

2. Eight out of ten children like maths more than any other subject.

   _____% of children like maths more than any other subject.

3. Four in five people read our newspaper!

   _____% of people read our newspaper!

4. Our football team won sixteen of their last twenty matches.

   Our football team won _____% of their last twenty matches.

Percentages

Learning objective: to find percentages of whole number quantities

Percentages are simply fractions out of 100. 'Per cent' means 'out of 100' and the percentage sign is %.

We often need to work out percentages of amounts.
For example, what is 20% of 60 metres?
In examples like this, 'of' means multiply, so this is 20% x 60.
Look at these two methods to work this out.

Method 1

If you can multiply fractions, change the percentage to a fraction and work it out:

$$20\% = \frac{20^1}{100^5} = \frac{1}{5} \quad \text{and} \quad 60m = \frac{60}{1}$$

$$\frac{1}{5} \times \frac{60}{1} = \frac{60^{12}}{5^1} = 12m$$

Method 2

The quick method is to use 10% to work it out. 10% is $\frac{1}{10}$, which is the same as dividing a number by 10:

10% of 60 is 6.

So, 20% of 60m is double that: 12m

A

Write these percentages as fractions in their lowest terms.

For example: $30\% = \frac{30}{100} = \frac{6}{20} = \frac{3}{10}$

1. 40% $\rule{1.5cm}{0.4pt}$ → $\rule{1.5cm}{0.4pt}$ → $\rule{1.5cm}{0.4pt}$

2. 80% $\rule{1.5cm}{0.4pt}$ → $\rule{1.5cm}{0.4pt}$ → $\rule{1.5cm}{0.4pt}$

3. 25% $\rule{1.5cm}{0.4pt}$ → $\rule{1.5cm}{0.4pt}$ → $\rule{1.5cm}{0.4pt}$

'Lowest terms' means using small numbers.

DEFINITION

percentage: This is a fraction out of 100, shown with a % sign.

B

These are the marks that Joseph scored in some maths tests. Change them all to percentages to work out which test he scored highest in and which was his lowest score.

Test	Score	Percentage
1	$\frac{7}{10}$	
2	$\frac{18}{20}$	
3	$\frac{4}{5}$	

Test	Score	Percentage
4	$\frac{21}{25}$	
5	$\frac{38}{50}$	

C

Write these amounts.

1. 10% of 70cm = _____

2. 30% of 90km = _____

3. 20% of 20 litres = _____

4. 40% of 30kg = _____

5. 50% of 70ml = _____

6. 25% of 80m = _____

7. 10% of 600g = _____

8. 50% of 400mm = _____

You can revise percentages and fractions on page 32.

D

This chart shows different percentages of each length. Complete the chart by writing in the missing lengths.

	50%	25%	10%	40%	5%
60m	30m				3m
50m		12.5m			
300m				120m	
250m			25m		

37

Proportion

Learning objective: to solve simple problems involving proportions of quantities

Finding the proportion of an amount is the same as finding the fraction of the whole amount. A proportion can be written as a fraction.

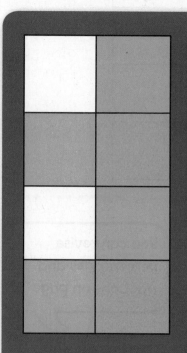

What proportion of the tiles are white?
When you look at the proportion of an amount, it is the same as finding the fraction of the whole amount.
There are 8 tiles altogether, 2 of them are white, so $\frac{2}{8}$ of the tiles are white.
This means that the proportion of white tiles is 1 in every 4, or $\frac{1}{4}$.

Two quantities are in direct proportion when they increase or decrease in the same ratio.
For example, if 3 apples weigh 300g, what is the weight of 15 apples?
This is 5 times the number of apples, so it is five times the weight: 300g x 5 = 1500g (or 1.5kg).

A Look at these tile patterns. What proportion of each of the patterns is blue?

1. ____   2. ____   3. ____   4. ____   5. ____   6. ____

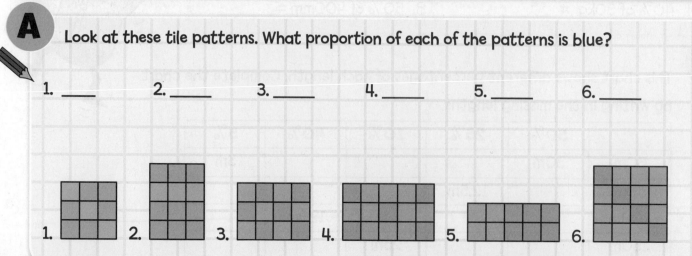

1.   2.   3.   4.   5.   6.

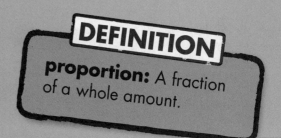
DEFINITION

proportion: A fraction of a whole amount.

B

Complete these tables showing the proportion of fruit in juice drinks.

The fruits are measured in fifths. The proportion of fruit stays the same in each table.

1.

Pineapples	Oranges	Total
1	4	5
2	8	
	20	
8		
10		

2.

Bananas	Peaches	Total
2	3	5
4	6	
	18	
16		
		50

C

In these recipes the amount of each ingredient is given as a proportion of the total weight.

Write the missing weights of each ingredient in these two recipes.

1. **600g Carrot and walnut cake**

$\frac{1}{4}$ butter   150g

$\frac{1}{3}$ flour   200g

$\frac{1}{6}$ grated carrots _____g

$\frac{1}{10}$ sugar _____g

$\frac{1}{12}$ beaten eggs _____g

$\frac{1}{15}$ walnuts _____g

2. **360g Chocolate chip cookies**

$\frac{1}{2}$ flour _____g

$\frac{1}{4}$ butter _____g

$\frac{1}{6}$ sugar _____g

$\frac{1}{12}$ chocolate chips _____g

D

What weight of ingredients are needed for a 1.2kg Carrot and walnut cake?

butter _____g

flour _____g

grated carrots _____g

sugar _____g

beaten eggs _____g

walnuts _____g

39

Learning objective: to describe the properties of polygons

Polygons are straight-sided, closed shapes. Quadrilaterals are any shapes with 4 straight sides.

Learn the properties of these different polygons.

Number of sides		Name	Number of sides		Name
3		Triangle	6		Hexagon
4		Quadrilateral	7		Heptagon
5		Pentagon	8		Octagon

Learn the properties of these different quadrilaterals.

Square
- 4 equal sides
- 4 right angles

Rectangle
- 2 pairs of equal sides
- 4 right angles

Rhombus
- 4 equal sides
- opposite angles equal
- opposite sides parallel

Parallelogram
- opposite sides are equal and parallel

Kite
- 2 pairs of adjacent sides that are equal

Trapezium
- 1 pair of parallel sides

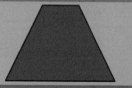

40

DEFINITION

adjacent: Being positioned next to something else.

DEFINITION

parallel: Two or more lines that are the same distance apart.

A

Count the sides and write the name for each shape.

1. _____

2. _____

3. _____

4. _____

5. _____

6. _____

2D means two-dimensional. Am I a 2D shape?

B

Name each of these quadrilaterals.

1. _____

2. _____

3. _____

4. _____

5. _____

6. _____

C

Complete these sentences by writing <u>always</u>, <u>sometimes</u> or <u>never</u>.

Look at the shapes on these two pages to help you.

1. A rectangle _____ has 4 right angles.

2. An octagon _____ has 7 sides.

3. The opposite sides of a parallelogram are _____ parallel.

4. The sides of a square are _____ equal.

5. A triangle _____ has a right angle.

6. The sides of a rhombus are _____ the same length.

41

Angles

Learning objective: to calculate angles in straight lines and triangles

The amount by which something turns is an angle.
Angles are measured in degrees (°). There are 360° in a circle.
These are some special angles to remember:

90° (right angle)

An acute angle is less than a right angle.

A device called a protractor can be used to measure angles.

180° (straight angle)

An obtuse angle is between 90° and 180°.

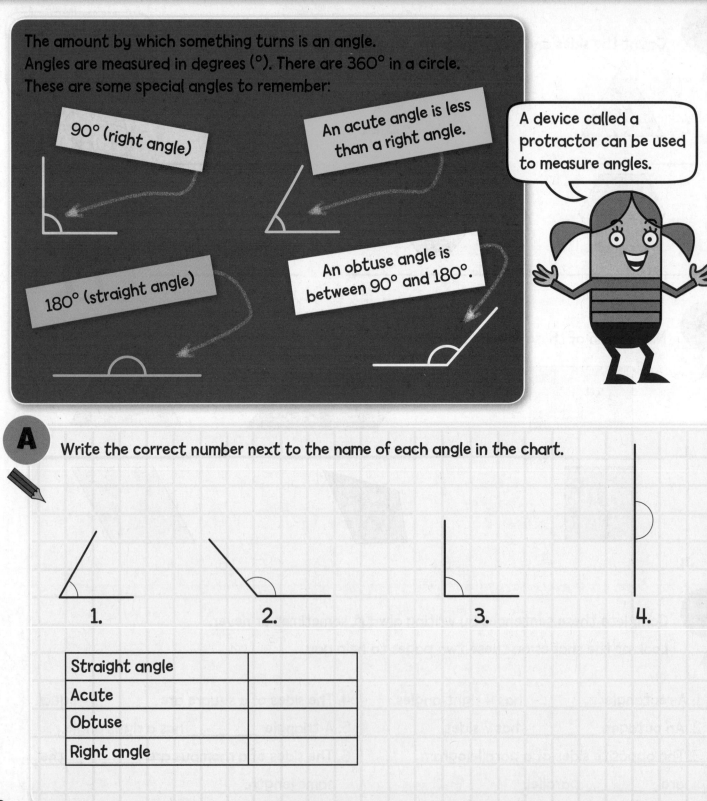

A Write the correct number next to the name of each angle in the chart.

1.   2.   3.   4.

Straight angle	
Acute	
Obtuse	
Right angle	

DEFINITION

angle: The space where two lines meet that measures how much one line turns away from the other.

B

Write the missing angle on these shapes. Angles in a triangle always add up to 180°.

1. 69° 68°

2. 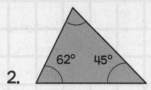 62° 45°

3. 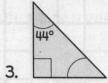 44°

C

Write the missing angles below. Angles in a straight line always add up to 180°.

1. 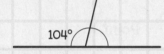 104°

2. 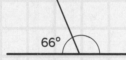 66°

3. 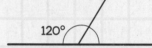 120°

4. 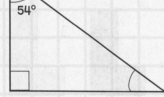 54°

5.  42°

6.  78°

D

Write the two missing angles on these.

1. 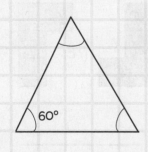 60°

2. 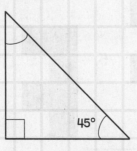 45°

Remember that a right angle always measures 90°.

Mo in s u

Learning objective: to draw shapes on grids after translation, reflection or rotation

A shape can be moved by translation, reflection or rotation.

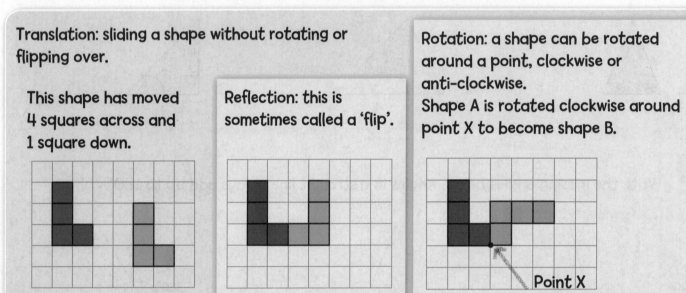

Translation: sliding a shape without rotating or flipping over.

This shape has moved 4 squares across and 1 square down.

Reflection: this is sometimes called a 'flip'.

Rotation: a shape can be rotated around a point, clockwise or anti-clockwise.
Shape A is rotated clockwise around point X to become shape B.

Point X

A Write whether these shapes have been translated, rotated or reflected.

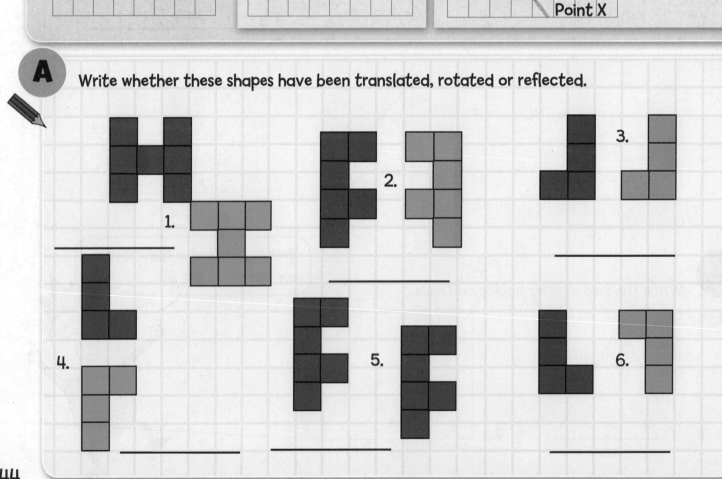

1.

2.

3.

4.

5.

6.

44

DEFINITION

clockwise: Moving in the same direction as the hands of a clock.

DEFINITION

anti-clockwise: Moving in the opposite direction to the hands of a clock.

B

Repeat these shape tiles to design a larger pattern.

Decide whether to rotate, reflect or translate each tile.

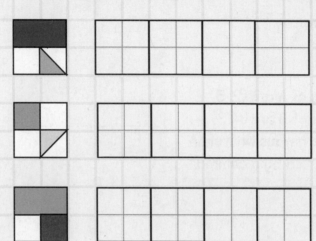

Can you make a symmetrical pattern?

C

Copy this tile and repeat it 10 times.

Use it to make a pattern of translated, rotated or reflected tiles.

Design your own tile and explore the patterns you can make.

Coordinates

Learning objective: to use coordinates to draw and find shapes

Coordinates are used to show an exact position of a point on a grid.
Two numbers from the x and y axes show the position.

> The number on the horizontal x axis is written first, then the vertical y axis. You can remember this because x comes before y in the alphabet!

Look at the graph.

The coordinates of A are (2, 5)
The coordinates of B are (4, 3)
Coordinates are always written in brackets separated by a comma.

A

DEFINITION

axis: The horizontal or vertical line on a graph. Plural is **axes**.

1. A, B and C are corners of a rectangle. What are the coordinates of the fourth corner?

2. P, Q and R are corners of a parallelogram. What are the coordinates of the fourth corner?

B

Look at how each of these triangles has moved. Write the coordinates of the vertices of all the triangles.

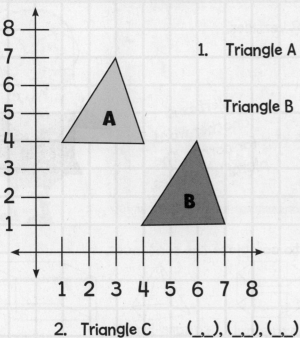

1. Triangle A   (1, 4), (3, 7), (4, 4)

    Triangle B   (_,_), (_,_), (_,_)

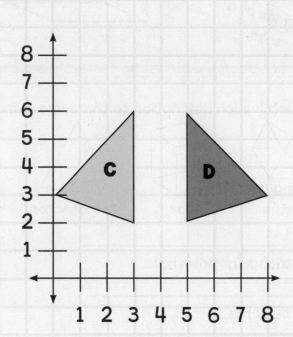

2. Triangle C   (_,_), (_,_), (_,_)

    Triangle D   (_,_), (_,_), (_,_)

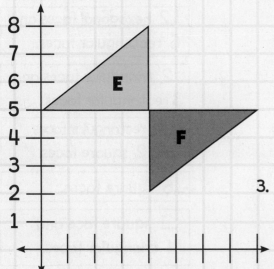

3. Triangle E   (_,_), (_,_), (_,_)

    Triangle F   (_,_), (_,_), (_,_)

3D Shapes

A solid shape has three dimensions: height, length and width.

Solid or 3D shapes are made up of faces, edges and vertices (corners).

A cuboid has 6 faces, 12 edges and 8 vertices.

An edge is where two faces meet.

A face is a flat surface of a solid.

Vertex is another word for corner. The plural is vertices.

What shape is a cereal box?

A Match each description to the shape name to complete the sentences.

triangular prism   cube   tetrahedron   hexagonal prism   square-based pyramid   cuboid

1. A triangular prism has...
2. A cube has...
3. A tetrahedron has...
4. A hexagonal prism has...
5. A square-based pyramid has...
6. A cuboid has...

...4 triangular faces.

...2 hexagonal faces and 6 rectangular faces.

...2 triangular faces and 3 rectangular faces.

...4 rectangular faces and 2 square faces.

...6 square faces.

...1 square face and 4 triangular faces.

Prisms

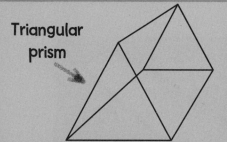

Triangular prism

Prisms have rectangular faces, with the shape of the end face giving each prism its name.

Cuboids and cubes are special types of prism.

Pyramids

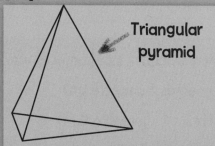

Triangular pyramid

The shape of the base gives each pyramid its name. The triangular faces of a pyramid all meet at a point.

Another name for a triangular pyramid is a tetrahedron.

B

Sort these shapes into prisms and pyramids. Complete the table below.

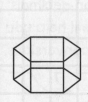

A

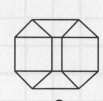

B

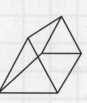

C

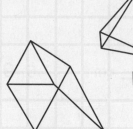

D

E

F

G

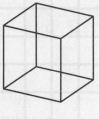

H

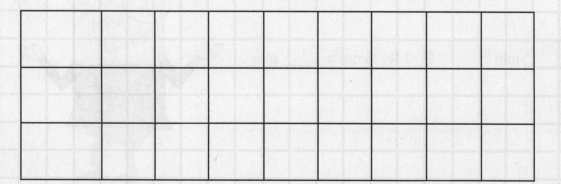

Measuring length

Learning objective: to convert units of length and measure lines accurately

We measure length using kilometres, metres, centimetres and millimetres.

10 millimetres (mm) = 1 centimetre (cm)

100 centimetres = 1 metre (m)

1000 metres = 1 kilometre (km)

2.8cm = 2cm 8mm = 28mm

3.45m = 3m 45cm = 345cm

6.5km = 6km 500m = 6500m

To measure the length of lines accurately you may need to use millimetres.

A Complete these.

1. 58 mm = _____ cm

2. 10.67 m = _____ cm

3. 910 cm = _____ m

4. 13.5 cm = _____ mm

5. 8.3 km = _____ m

6. 94 mm = _____ cm

7. 3700 m = _____ km

8. 14.6 cm = _____ mm

Your work on decimals on page 6 will help you with these conversions.

B

Use a ruler to measure the length of each line accurately in millimetres.

1. _____   4. _____

2. _____   5. _____

3. _____   6. _____

C

The perimeter of a shape is the distance all around the edge.
These shapes are all regular, so each side is the same length.

Measure the length of one side of each shape in
millimetres. Use this measurement to work out
the perimeter of each shape.

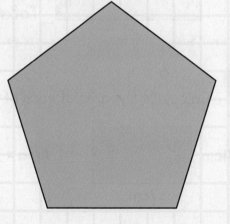

1.

= _____ mm

2.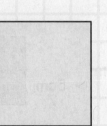

= _____ mm

3.

= _____ mm

4.

= _____ mm

Use millimetres when you
need to measure something
accurately.

51

Area

Learning objective: to be able to calculate the area of a shape

The area of a shape is the amount of surface that it covers.

The area of a rectangle or square can be calculated by multiplying the length by the width.

4cm

6cm

6cm x 4cm = 24cm²

Area is measured in square units, such as square centimetres (cm²) and square metres (m²).

The area of shapes made from rectangles can be found by working out the area of each part.

4cm

4cm

3cm

2cm

3 x 4 = 12cm²
2 x 4 = 8cm²
Total area = 20cm²

A

Calculate the area of each of these.

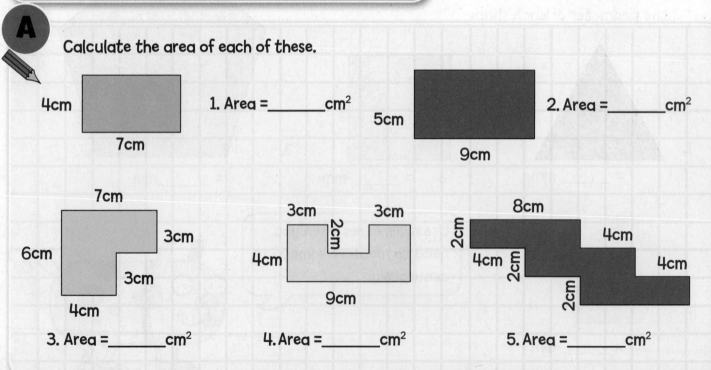

4cm

7cm

1. Area = _____ cm²

5cm

9cm

2. Area = _____ cm²

7cm

3cm

6cm

3cm

4cm

3. Area = _____ cm²

3cm   3cm

2cm

4cm

9cm

4. Area = _____ cm²

8cm

2cm

4cm

4cm

2cm

2cm

4cm

2cm

5. Area = _____ cm²

To find the area (a) of a triangle, multiply the base (b) by the height (h) then divide by 2.

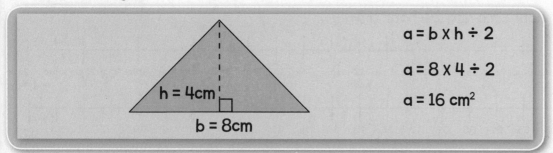

$a = b \times h \div 2$

$a = 8 \times 4 \div 2$

$a = 16 \text{ cm}^2$

h = 4cm

b = 8cm

To find the area (a) of a parallelogram, multiply the base (b) by the height (h).

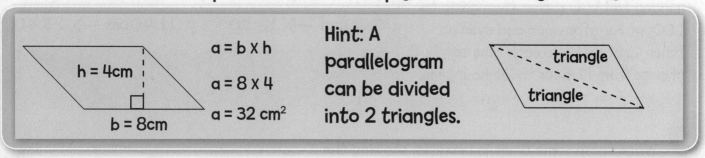

h = 4cm

b = 8cm

$a = b \times h$

$a = 8 \times 4$

$a = 32 \text{ cm}^2$

Hint: A parallelogram can be divided into 2 triangles.

triangle

triangle

B Calculate the area of each of these.

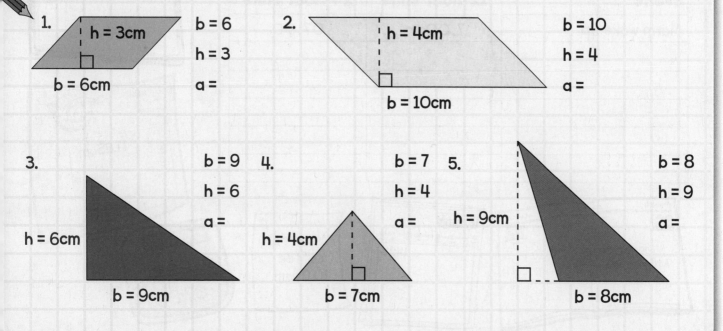

1. h = 3cm

b = 6cm

b = 6
h = 3
a =

2. h = 4cm

b = 10cm

b = 10
h = 4
a =

3. h = 6cm

b = 9cm

b = 9
h = 6
a =

4. h = 4cm

b = 7cm

b = 7
h = 4
a =

5. h = 9cm

b = 8cm

b = 8
h = 9
a =

Time

Learning objective: to read the time using 24-hour clock notation and read Roman numerals

Timetables and digital watches often use the 24-hour clock.

This line compares 12-hour time and 24-hour time.

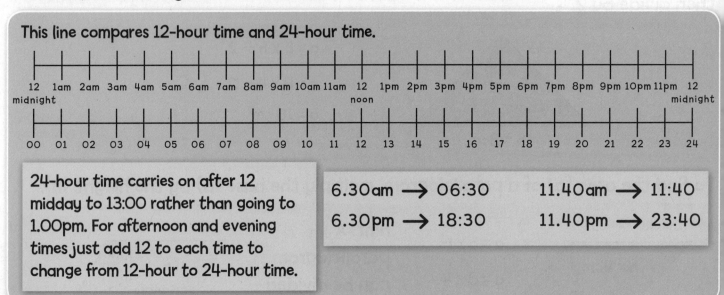

| 12 midnight | 1am | 2am | 3am | 4am | 5am | 6am | 7am | 8am | 9am | 10am | 11am | 12 noon | 1pm | 2pm | 3pm | 4pm | 5pm | 6pm | 7pm | 8pm | 9pm | 10pm | 11pm | 12 midnight |

| 00 | 01 | 02 | 03 | 04 | 05 | 06 | 07 | 08 | 09 | 10 | 11 | 12 | 13 | 14 | 15 | 16 | 17 | 18 | 19 | 20 | 21 | 22 | 23 | 24 |

24-hour time carries on after 12 midday to 13:00 rather than going to 1.00pm. For afternoon and evening times just add 12 to each time to change from 12-hour to 24-hour time.

6.30am → 06:30   11.40am → 11:40
6.30pm → 18:30   11.40pm → 23:40

A  Write these same times in two lists, showing the times as both 24-hour and 12-hour times.

Event	12-hour time	24-hour time
Alarm wake up	7.00am	07:00

taxi 7.15pm

11.35am

19:40 Amazing Maths

14:18

Meet for coffee 10.00am

07:00

am: 'Ante meridiem'
meaning 'before midday'.
pm: 'Post meridiem'
meaning 'after midday'.

We sometimes see letters instead of numbers on clocks and watches.
These are called Roman numerals.

Both these clocks show a time of quarter past 5.

Remember!
IX = 9 (10–1)
XL = 40 (50–10)

Here are more Roman numerals that you need to know:

XX	20	CC	200
XXX	30	CCC	300
XL	40	CD	400
L	50	D	500
LX	60	DC	600
LXX	70	DCC	700
LXXX	80	DCCC	800
XC	90	CM	900
C	100	M	1000

B

Write these numbers as Roman numerals. The first one has been done for you.

1. 23 = __XXIII__

2. 79 = _____

3. 105 = _____

4. 55 = _____

5. 240 = _____

6. 999 = _____

C

Translate these Roman numerals into numbers. The first one has been done for you.

1. CL = __150__

2. LXV = _____

3. XCVI = _____

4. CLXII = _____

5. CCX = _____

6. ML = _____

D

1. In Roman numerals, write the year you were born: _____

2. In Roman numerals, write the year now: _____

Data

Learning objective: to solve problems using the mode, median and mean

Averages are middle scores or the most common numbers.
There are three main types of average: mean, mode and median.

> When working out the median and there is an even amount of numbers, you take the two middle numbers, add them together and divide by two.

Look at this example to compare the three types of average.
This chart shows the goals scored by the players in a football team.
Does Sam score above the average number of goals for the team?

Player	Sam	Brent	Jason	Ali	Carl
Goals scored	8	4	8	6	9

Mode is the most common number.
2 players scored 8 goals so that is the mode.

Median is the middle number when listed in order - 4, 6, 8, 8, 9.
8 is the median number of goals.

For the mean, add the numbers and divide the total by the number of items in the list.
$4 + 6 + 8 + 8 + 9 = 35$ $35 \div 5 = 7$
So the mean average is 7 goals.

Sam is an above-average goal scorer compared with the mean average,
and at the average for the mode and median.

A   A packet of fruit-drops is divided into piles of different flavours.

grape (purple) = 3	lemon (yellow) = 4	strawberry (pink) = 7
orange (orange) = 4	lime (green) = 8	raspberry (red) = 4

1. Which is the most common amount of sweets of the same flavour? _____

   Is this the mean, mode or median? _____

2. If the piles of sweets were put in order of size, which size pile would be in the middle?

   _____

   Is this the mean, mode or median? _____

B

These are the heights of a group of five children.

| Ben: 140cm | Sam: 130cm | Eve: 140cm | Amy: 150cm | Jon: 190cm |

1. What is the mode height?

2. What is the median height?

3. What is the mean height?

4. How many children are above the mean average height?

5. Which child is at the mean average height?

6. Another child joins the group. Her height is 120cm. What is the mean average height for the group now?

Remember!
Mode is the most common number.

C

These are the hand-spans for a group of 10 children.

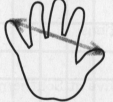

A hand-span is measured from the tip of the little finger to the tip of the thumb.

| 10cm | 8cm | 12cm | 9cm | 8cm | 10cm | 13cm | 11cm | 9cm | 10cm |

1. Median: _____   2. Mode: _____   3. Mean: _____

Challenge

Read this graph and find the median, mode and mean averages of the number of hours of TV watched each day in one week.

hours

10
8
6
4
2
0

Mon   Tue   Wed   Thur   Fri   Sat   Sun

4. Median: _____   5. Mode: _____   6. Mean: _____

57

Learning objective: to be able to read timetables and other charts, and answer questions about them

A timetable tells you what is happening and when, such as the times of trains, buses and other public transport. Timetables are set out in columns.

Highton to Southern Airport train timetable

Highton	08:10	08:30	09:05
Cove	08:20	08:40	09:15
Farthing	08:45	....	....
Newchester	09:05	09:20	09:55
Fisham	09:55	....	....
Seabay	10:10	10:20	10:55
Southern Airport	10:30	10:40	11:15

A

Use the timetable above to answer the questions.

1. What time does the 08:10 from Highton arrive at Southern Airport? _____

2. Does the 08:30 from Highton stop at Farthing? _____

3. What time does the 08:30 from Highton arrive at Newchester? _____

4. You are at Highton and you need to get to Seabay for 10:15. Which train would you get? _____

5. You arrive at Cove at 08:30. How long do you have to wait for a train to the airport? _____

6. How long does it take the 09:05 from Highton to reach the airport? _____

I wonder what train I need to get to arrive at the airport in time to catch my flight?

DEFINITION

time zone: The world is divided into 24 time zones because different places on Earth have daylight at different times.

Southern Airport departures timetable

Destination Airport	Departs	Arrives	Comments
Athens	13:15	16:55	Delayed by 45 minutes
Berlin	13:30	15:20	
Cape Town	14:00	01:30	
Paris	14:10	15:30	
Los Angeles	14:15	01:30	
Reykjavik	14:25	17:30	Delayed by 25 minutes
Warsaw	14:30	16:55	

B Use the timetable above to answer the questions. (The arrival time is given according to the same time zone as the departure time.)

1. The longest flight is to _____. It takes ____ hours ___ minutes

2. The shortest flight is to _____. It takes ____ hour ___ minutes

3. How long is the flight to Los Angeles? _____

4. What time will the Athens flight arrive, given the delay? _____

C

12:00 (pm) midnight London, UK, compared to worldwide times:

London	00:00
Dubai	04:00 (ahead)
New York	19:00 (behind)
Singapore	08:00 (ahead)
Sydney	11:00 (ahead)
Vancouver	16:00 (behind)

Use this world time chart to answer the questions.

1. It is 12:00 noon in London. What time is it in New York? _____

2. What is the time difference between London and Singapore? _____

3. It is 21:00 in London. What time is it in Sydney? _____

4. It is midnight in New York. What time is it in London? _____

Answers

Pages 6-7

A
1. 0.2   8. 8.79
2. 0.35   9. 8.95
3. 0.71   10. 16.18
4. 0.96   11. 16.4
5. 8.18   12. 16.53
6. 8.4   13. 16.79
7. 8.53   14. 16.99

B
Leatherback turtle   462.9kg
Green sea turtle   355.3kg
Loggerhead turtle   257.801kg
Flatback turtle   78.151kg
Hawksbill turtle   62.65kg
Kemp's Ridley turtle   60.45kg

C 2. 3.58, 3.85, 5.38, 5.83, 8.35, 8.53

Pages 8-9

A
1. 13.5   3. 6.85
2. 96.75   4. 33.46

B
1. 35 litres   3. 25kg
2. 98.52km

C
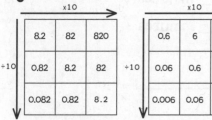

	x10		
÷10	8.2	82	820
	0.82	8.2	82
	0.082	0.82	8.2

	x10		
÷10	0.6	6	60
	0.06	0.6	6
	0.006	0.06	0.6

Pages 10-11

A
1. 6   2. 16   3. 7   4. 18
5. 9   6. 12   7. 5   8. 6
9. 7   10. 63   11. 9   12. 6

B
1. 20   2. 5   3. 16   4. 11
5. 12   6. 5   7. 2   8. 47

C
1. 19 - (12 - 5) = 12
2. 16 - (10 - 6) = 12
3. 22 - (5 + 5) = 12
4. (6 + 13) - 7 = 12
   or 6 + (13 - 7) = 12
5. (24 - 6) - 6 = 12
6. 20 - (10 - 2) = 12

D
1. 48   2. 7   3. 8
4. 21   5. 9   6. 20

Pages 12-13

A and B

	0	1	2	3	4	5	6	7	8	9	10	11	12
0	0	0	0	0	0	0	0	0	0	0	0	0	0
1	0	1	2	3	4	5	6	7	8	9	10	11	12
2	0	2	4	6	8	10	12	14	16	18	20	22	24
3	0	3	6	9	12	15	18	21	24	27	30	33	36
4	0	4	8	12	16	20	24	28	32	36	40	44	48
5	0	5	10	15	20	25	30	35	40	45	50	55	60
6	0	6	12	18	24	30	36	42	48	54	60	66	72
7	0	7	14	21	28	35	42	49	56	63	70	77	84
8	0	8	16	24	32	40	48	56	64	72	80	88	96
9	0	9	18	27	36	45	54	63	72	81	90	99	108
10	0	10	20	30	40	50	60	70	80	90	100	110	120
11	0	11	22	33	44	55	66	77	88	99	110	121	132
12	0	12	24	36	48	60	72	84	96	108	120	132	144

C
1. 24, 48   4. 18, 77
2. 15, 12   5. 6, 50
3. 46   6. 39, 92

D
1. 16   6. 4
2. 49   7. 100
3. 36   8. 9
4. 81   9. 64
5. 144   10. 25

Pages 14-15

A
1. (1, 8) (2, 4)
2. (1, 20) (2, 10) (4, 5)
3. (1, 24) (2, 12) (3, 8) (4, 6)
4. (1, 28) (2, 14) (4, 7)

B
1. 4, 8, 12, 16, 20, 24, 28, 32, 36, 40
2. 3, 6, 9, 12, 15, 18, 21, 24, 27, 30
3. 6, 12, 18, 24, 30, 36, 42, 48, 54, 60
4. 5, 10, 15, 20, 25, 30, 35, 40, 45, 50
5. 10, 20, 30, 40, 50, 60, 70, 80, 90, 100
6. 8, 16, 24, 32, 40, 48, 56, 64, 72, 80

C
1. 15, 30   2. 12, 24
3. 20, 40   4. 24, 48
5. 30, 60   6. 12, 24, 36

D

Factor of 24 | Multiple of 3

10, 2, 4, 1, 16 (Factor of 24 only)
3, 12, 24, 6 (intersection)
15, 20, 9, 30, 18, 25 (Multiple of 3 only)

Pages 16-17

A
1. The number 5 cannot be divided by 2 or 3 or 4.
So the number 5 is prime.
2. The number 6 can be divided by 2 or 3. So the number 6 is not prime.
3. The number 7 cannot be divided by 2 or 3 or 4 or 5 or 6. So the number 7 is prime.
4. The number 3 cannot be divided by 2. So the number 3 is prime.
5. The number 8 can be divided by 2 or 4. So the number 8 is not prime.
6. The number 11 cannot be divided by 2 or 3 or 4 or 5 or 6 or 7 or 8 or 9 or 10. So the number 11 is prime.

B The hidden primes are: 7, 11, 13, 17, 19, 23, 29

C They can't be divided whatever you do.
The smallest prime is number two.
Then come three and five and seven.
The next prime is of course eleven.
Thirteen is next upon the scene.
Seventeen follows, and then nineteen.

Pages 18-19

A
1. 9468
2. 7803
3. 4479

B
1. 9625   4. 7869
2. 9803   5. 7077
3. 6078   6. 6435

C
1. 3420km   4. 4849km
2. 5803km   5. 4490km
3. 6281km

D
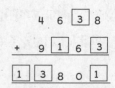

```
      4   6  [3]  8
  +   9  [1]  6  [3]
  [1] [3]  8   0  [1]
```

Pages 20-21

A
1. 3146   2. 5668
3. 4370

B
1. 3847 - 1762 = 2085
2. 7943 - 2486 = 5457
3. 4115 - 2936 = 1179

1. 1161m

2. 1381m

3. 1279m

4. Caribbean and Bering

5. Caribbean

6. Indian and Atlantic

Pages 22-23

1. 1444   2. 3108

3. 456   4. 3286

1. 720 hours   3. 700g

2. 928km   4. 735

Items	Amount in 1 pack	Number of packs	Total number of items
Pencils	28	76	2128
Chalk	15	33	495
Sharpeners	26	19	494
Erasers	48	14	672
Pens	52	58	3016
Crayons	34	47	1598

1. $543 \times 6 = 3258$

2. $456 \times 3 = 1368$

3. $456 \times 3 = 1368$

Pages 24-25

1. 162 r2   3. 47 r1

2. 73 r2   4. 231 r2

1 ⟶ $271 \div 6$

2 ⟶ $608 \div 3$

3 ⟶ $315 \div 8$

4 ⟶ $454 \div 5$

5 ⟶ $149 \div 6$

6 ⟶ $398 \div 7$

7 ⟶ $259 \div 9$

8 ⟶ $458 \div 9$

9 ⟶ $359 \div 10$

Day of the week	Number of Eggs collected	Full boxes (6 eggs)	Eggs left over
Monday	627	104	3
Tuesday	572	95	2
Wednesday	700	116	4
Thursday	644	107	2
Friday	683	113	5
Saturday	594	99	0
Sunday	735	122	3

Pages 26-27

A
1. $a + 30 = 100$

$a + 30 - 30 = 100 - 30$

$a = 70$

2. $a + 20 = 80$

$a + 20 - 20 = 80 - 20$

$a = 60$

3. $a - 40 = 120$

$a - 40 + 40 = 120 + 40$

$a = 160$

4. $a - 100 = 150$

$a - 100 + 100 = 150 + 100$

$a = 250$

B
1. $b \times 12 = 48$

$b \times 12 \div 12 = 48 \div 12$

$b = 4$

2. $b \times 30 = 120$

$b \times 30 \div 30 = 120 \div 30$

$b = 4$

3. $b \div 8 = 9$

$b \div 8 \times 8 = 9 \times 8$

$b = 72$

4. $b \div 10 = 15$

$b \div 10 \times 10 = 15 \times 10$

$b = 150$

C
1. $2 \times 20 + 9 = 49$

2. $2q + 4 = 10$

$2q + 4 - 4 = 10 - 4$

$2q = 6$

$2q \div 2 = 6 \div 2$

$q = 3$

Pages 28-29

A Liverpool – 469000

Bradford – 293700

Sheffield – 439900

Derby – 229400

Birmingham – 970900

Nottingham – 249600

Bristol – 420600

Plymouth – 243800

B
1. 800   4. 1200

2. 500   5. 5900

3. 100   6. 13700

C
1. 16kg   2. 21kg

3. 34kg   4. 45kg

D
1. 0.93   2. 7.08

3. 12.95   4. 7.59

5. 2.91   6. 30.08

Pages 30-31

A
1. 67.83   3. 91.81

2. 84.76   4. 85.51

B
1. 43.02   3. 37.76

2. 47.23   4. 41.78

C
1. 26.63 l   3. 68.01kg

2. 63.91m   4. 81.23m

D
1. 0.76   4. 0.09

2. 0.51   5. 1.34

3. Eileen and Nikki

Pages 32-33

A
1. $15 \div 5 = 3$ $40 \div 5 = 8$

So $\frac{15}{40}$ is the same as $\frac{3}{8}$

2. $14 \div 2 = 7$ $16 \div 2 = 8$

So $\frac{14}{16}$ is the same as $\frac{7}{8}$

3. $8 \div 4 = 2$ $12 \div 4 = 3$

So $\frac{8}{12}$ is the same as $\frac{2}{3}$

4. $20 \div 10 = 2$ $30 \div 10 = 3$

So $\frac{20}{30}$ is the same as $\frac{2}{3}$

B
1. $\frac{5}{9} + \frac{8}{9} = \frac{13}{9} = 1\frac{4}{9}$

2. $\frac{7}{10} + \frac{8}{10} = \frac{15}{10} = \frac{3}{2} = 1\frac{1}{2}$

C
1. $\frac{1}{3} + \frac{1}{9} = \frac{3}{9} + \frac{1}{9} = \frac{4}{9}$

2. $\frac{3}{7} + \frac{1}{14} = \frac{6}{14} + \frac{1}{14} = \frac{7}{14} = \frac{1}{2}$

3. $\frac{1}{3} + \frac{1}{2} = \frac{2}{6} + \frac{3}{6} = \frac{5}{6}$

4. $\frac{1}{2} + \frac{3}{5} = \frac{5}{10} + \frac{6}{10} = \frac{11}{10} = 1\frac{1}{10}$

5. $\frac{7}{9} - \frac{1}{3} = \frac{7}{9} - \frac{3}{9} = \frac{4}{9}$

6. $\frac{2}{3} - \frac{1}{4} = \frac{8}{12} - \frac{3}{12} = \frac{5}{12}$

Answers

Pages 34-35

A
1. 30% 5. 80%
2. 20% 6. 10%
3. 7%   7. 65%
4. 22% 8. 12%

B
1. 0.5 4. 5 (to make $\frac{2}{5}$)
2. 25% 5. 0.34
3. 5%   6. 70%

Pages 34-35 continued

C
1. $\frac{1}{4}$, 25%   4. $\frac{3}{10}$, 30%
2. $\frac{4}{8}$, 50%   5. $\frac{2}{5}$, 40%
3. $\frac{7}{10}$, 70% 6. $\frac{4}{8}$, 50%

D
1. 1%   3. 80%
2. 80% 4. 80%

Pages 36-37

A
1. $\frac{2}{5}$ 2. $\frac{4}{5}$ 3. $\frac{1}{4}$

B
1. 70% 4. 84%
2. 90% 5. 76%
3. 80%

C
1. 7cm   5. 35ml
2. 27km   6. 20m
3. 4 litres 7. 60g
4. 12kg   8. 200mm

D

	50%	25%	10%	40%	5%
60m	30m	15m	6m	24m	3m
50m	25m	12.5m	5m	20m	2.5m
300m	150m	75m	30m	120m	15m
250m	125m	62.5m	25m	100m	12.5m

Pages 38-39

A
1. $\frac{1}{3}$ 2. $\frac{1}{4}$

3. $\frac{1}{2}$ 4. $\frac{2}{3}$

5. $\frac{2}{5}$ 6. $\frac{3}{4}$

B

1.
Pineapples	Oranges	Total
1	4	5
2	8	10
5	20	25
8	32	40
10	40	50

2.
Bananas	Peaches	Total
2	3	5
4	6	10
12	18	30
16	24	40
20	30	50

Pages 38-39 continued

C
1. butter 150g   sugar 60g
   flour 200g   eggs 50g
   carrots 100g   walnuts 40g
2. flour 180g   butter 90g
   sugar 60g   choc chips 30g

D butter 300g   sugar 120g
   flour 400g   eggs 100g
   carrots 200g   walnuts 80g

Pages 40-41

A
1. triangle   4. hexagon
2. quadrilateral 5. heptagon
3. pentagon   6. octagon

B
1. rectangle   4. square
2. parallelogram 5. kite
3. trapezium   6. rhombus

C
1. always   4. always
2. never   5. sometimes
3. always   6. always

Pages 42-43

A

Straight angle	4
Acute	1
Obtuse	2
Right angle	3

B
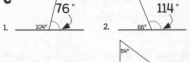

C
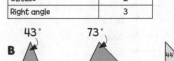

D
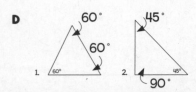

62

Pages 44-45

A 1. rotated   2. reflected
    3. translated   4. reflected
    5. translated   6. rotated

Pages 46-47

A 1. (3, 5)   2. (8, 8)

B 1. Triangle B
    (4, 1) (6, 4) (7, 1)
   2. Triangle C
    (0, 3) (3, 2) (3, 6)
    Triangle D
    (5, 2) (5, 6) (8, 3)
   3. Triangle E
    (0, 5) (4, 5) (4, 8)
    Triangle F
    (4, 2) (4, 5) (8, 5)

Pages 48-49

A 1. A triangular prism has 2
    triangular faces and 3
    rectangular faces.
   2. A cube has 6 square faces.
   3. A tetrahedron has 4 triangular faces.
   4. A hexagonal prism has 2
    hexagonal faces and 6
    rectangular faces.
   5. A square-based pyramid has 1 square
    face and 4 triangular faces.
   6. A cuboid has 4 rectangular faces and
    2 square faces.

B

	A	B	C	D	E	F	G	H
Prism	✔	✔	✔	✔	✔			✔
Pyramid						✔	✔	

Pages 50-51

A 1. 5.8cm   2. 1067cm
   3. 9.1m   4. 135mm
   5. 8300m   6. 9.4cm
   7. 3.7km   8. 146mm

B 1. 35mm   2. 52mm
   3. 26mm   4. 18mm
   5. 63mm   6. 37mm

C 1. 108mm   2. 112mm
   3. 175mm   4. 96mm

Pages 52-53

A 1. $28cm^2$ 2. $45cm^2$
   3. $33cm^2$ 4. $30cm^2$
   5. $48cm^2$

B 1. $18cm^2$ 2. $40cm^2$
   3. $27cm^2$ 4. $14cm^2$
   5. $36cm^2$

Pages 54-55

A Meet for coffee - 10.00am, 10:00
   Dentist - 11.35am, 11:35
   Bus time - 2.18pm, 14:18
   Taxi - 7.15pm, 19:15
   Amazing Maths - 7.40pm, 19:40

B 1. XXIII   4. LV
   2. LXXIX   5. CCXL
   3. CV   6. CMXCIX

C 1. 150   4. 162
   2. 65   5. 210
   3. 96   6. 1050

Pages 56-57

A 1. 4/mode
   2. 4/median

B 1. 140cm   4. 1
   2. 140cm   5. Amy
   3. 150cm   6. 145cm

C 1. Median 10cm
   2. Mode 10cm
   3. Mean 10cm
   Challenge
   4. Median 2 hours
   5. Mode 2 hours
   6. Mean 3 hours

Page 58-59

A 1. 10:30   2. No
   3. 09:20   4. 08:10
   5. 10 mins   6. 2 hrs 10 mins

B 1. Cape Town 11 hrs 30 mins
   2. Paris 1 hr 20 mins
   3. 11 hrs 15 mins
   4. 17:40

C 1. 07:00   2. 8 hrs
   3. 08:00   4. 05:00

Note for parent: For the purpose of these exercises, flight times are approximate and London times are based on British Summer time.

Notes